Frogs T...

By Liza Charlesworth

ISBN: 978-1-339-02667-1

Art Director: Tannaz Fassihi; Designer: Tanya Chernyak
Photos ©: p5: funstarts33/Shutterstock.com. All other photos © Getty Images.
Copyright © Liza Charlesworth. All rights reserved. Published by Scholastic Inc.

3 4 5 6 7 8 9 10   68   32 31 30 29 28 27 26 25 24

Printed in Jiaxing, China. First printing, August 2023.

See the frog on the frog.
Frogs can do a lot of tricks!

A frog can go on a trip!
It can hop on big rocks.

A frog can grin on a brick.

It can grip a stick.

Can a frog grab a bug?
Yes! Zip, zap, yum!

Drip, drop!
See the frog NOT get wet.

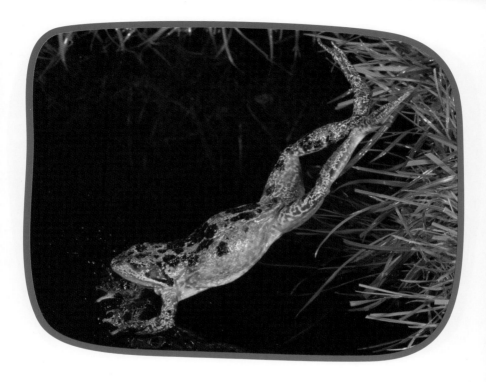

See the frog hop from the grass and get in a pond. Dip!

A frog is not drab.
It can do a lot of tricks!